Half Agony, Half Hope

Hannah Wilkinson

DEDICATION

To Jane and the Universe:
Thank you.

To the stag, the sailboat, the sunflower, the flying pig, and the butterfly,
I love you all so much.

"I can listen no longer in silence. I must speak to you by such means as are within my reach. You pierce my soul. I am half agony, half hope. Tell me not that I am too late, that such precious feelings are gone forever...
I have loved none but you."
-Jane Austen, *Persuasion*

CONTENTS

*"Tell me not that I am too late, that such
precious feelings are gone forever."*

"I have loved none but you."

Foreword

What follows is
my attempt at
breaking my own cycle.
They called me—
Boy Crazy
as far as I can remember:
Ticklish at the knees,
Addicted to limerence,
Dopamine junkie,
Chronic LTR heartbreaker,
Ship jumper,
Hopeless romantic.
Pushing my luck,
with serendipity
with fate.
My soul mates like a rabbit.
My heart breaks and breaks me.
Euphoric and suicidal.
I do it again.
I do it again.
I do it again.

"I can listen no longer in silence. I must speak
to you by such means as are within my reach."

If I Push Back, It Will Fall.

I'm afraid to ask for more
because I know my pride
will turn asking to telling
and your walls will thrust up against me
sending hot oil and how dare you
down my spine over burns and burns
and pleas to stay the night
or the year, not forever
and not for certain, but near enough
for blood to share and to poison
and to pump in perpetuity
for the one cause we both believe in
without actually standing behind

Circuit

I forgive you, you know?
I hope you know that.
It was a bad, bad thing that happened to me
and it altered me for good and bad.
It hurt like hell.
Sometimes I still vaguely hurt
even though the emotions are gone.
I did break.
I have had to be rebuilt
and I'm still building,
still broken,
still breaking,
still building,
in cycles.

Dropping Daisies

I'm dropping daisies, dropping down
back down where things are normal
where flashes dance upon my skin
out through my heavy eyelids
to break, to mark, to hunt again

(Probably Not The) Last Rites

I wanted you to hear me
when we were apart
to know that I loved you
when the world was
so heavy

It was a guilty pleasure
the injustice of it all
two twin souls torn apart
by circumstance, by time,
by promises

Made to those from before
those that didn't deserve
or those that didn't understand
our infinitely special, tender and fragile
pure oneness

Yet we seemed to know in an instant
how much of our everything
was nothing at all, in fact
that handful of departure just
fell away

And we became I, I severed
trudging along in tall britches
to start my new life, free,
tending to wounds, published,
year delayed

And I didn't think of you
once, I washed my hands of you
once, but I wasn't strong at all,
not for lack of you, it's just
my nature

I have been kicking
the life right out of me
pulling strings and setting
my entire world on fire
for regrowth

Nothing is the same as it was
and that is a good thing
but I still lie in vivisection
without a real plan
just bleeding

I don't miss you at all
but I'm still cursed to wonder
if you can hear me now, as
we are so apart, and the world is
so heavy

For all that has been
cast aside or replaced
I believe the twin souls hold true
and for that, you have my
sympathy

I want nothing more
than to tear our souls apart
by circumstance, by time, by promises
and I will keep trying to pry
you away

For now, you come up every day
and I resent your place on
the first pages of this new book
when you're not where I'm choosing to keep
my focus

If I were asked to describe
my most severe torments, they
would have to be more specific.
You're so small in the greater
scheme of things

Yet here you are, and
there you always were but
I do not want to do this
anymore. I'd rather put this
in the ground

When people leave this life
we don't get to know what
happened to them, indeed
we don't know if anything happens
anyway

We are meant to rely on faith
as a comfort that souls
go on to a better place
but they don't make faith for
things like this

Closure isn't real and the truth is
I have been leaving pieces of
me in so many places
that I wouldn't know which
door to close

My life is a hallway of open, bleeding doors?
If that's true, I built it myself
and everything is just as I left it
and I'm another year late to
fix anything

I hold no stock in my ability
to keep up with a tradition
but something has started today
in my ability to lie down and
hold a pen

Tonight I feel, and tonight
I acknowledge your loss
that something treasured is
now gone. Tonight I begin
Mourning #1

Propaganda

I am a propagandist
and I am the mislead masses
penning lines to my own audience
forcing a new truth in front of my eyes
worn like rose-colored glasses
through which you are falling in love
with my unique and irresistible spirit
and can it be helped with such
Unquestionable Chemistry?
Calling cosmic predictions and suspicions
of soul mates straight out of fiction
and it's that fiction that breaks the spell
and speaks harsh whispers to prove
that I've been a fool and that
I've made myself ridiculous
and can it be denied that you
can't stand the sight of me
and is there not evidence
that I make you uneasy?
Is there evidence of anything?
If I take down the posters
and projections and penny articles
what remains there other than
proof that I never broke the surface
and that none of it was real.
You were just part of my nightmare
and I can't fault you for that
any more than for being part
of my dreams in the first place.

The Lonely Sailor

I found a book of poetry
half eaten by mice
in an old kitchen drawer

it was handwritten,
a blank journal from 1969
the empty book, it said

I did not know the author
but he knew me, penned us
in flowing cursive ink

over two years of writing
his heart transitioned
from love to obsession

he couldn't have her
despite their everything
and it consumed him

I could have told him
that the old everything
will always win

that no amount of
collective dissatisfaction
will ever tip the scales.

my advice to a story written
in nineteen seventy one
seventy two seventy three

and that's when it got me
what fools we both were
building our unique tragedy

our cliches predate us both
just as they came before
this man lost his everything

as they will follow on
and infect some other pair
of unjust lovers

and when I think of that
eternal cycle of pure passion
and total devastation

I break for you, for them
for all that ends unwell and
all was and will be unwell

and I am unwell.

But has it ever been any different?

Ages

a thousand years ago
my feet wrapped up through
stars from down below
a thousand years ago
a drive for miles and hours
and hours to late
too late to hesitate
to meet the hand
and bring the hand to face
a thousand years ago
It can't be.
I know.

Oath of Service

Believing was easy.
Sign the dotted line. Yes.
Have my life. Sold. Enlisted.
I spoke the oath, hand on heart.

Reporting was easy.
Be there every day. Yes.
There for everything. Yours. Devoted.
I spoke the oath, hand on heart.

Hand on heart, I felt the cold.
Stunned. Yours. Resisted in everything.
No. You can't stay here.
Dismissal was easy.

Hand on heart, I shouted alarm.
Protested. Sold. Have my life.
No. Accept my decision.
That is impossible.

I spoke the oath, hand on heart.
Hand on heart, I scream.

I wrote you a song
and it is the air in which I live and breathe

I don't care what I said.
I'll always love you,
like that, like this,
like every other way I can.

Because I am yours, always,
and you occupy my heart.
You won all of me,
and all of my devotion,
without even trying.

You crossed the finish line
the moment you joined the race
and made me yours
in more ways than you intended.

Some things you can't take back
and as I've given you myself,
I can't take back myself,
and I've lost myself,
as I lost you.

You've made it clear
I have lost you
in all ways but one,
and believe me, I cherish that one.

You forever hold my Self,
and so to be myself
is to be near you.
To be near you is to be alive.

I sustain in this hollow,
bound by limits I must accept
to keep breathing, moving forward.
Your will moves the blood through my veins.

I will go on, for you.
I will find my own life, for you.
If what you want is my happiness,
I will be happy.

I am inexorably yours.

Thanks for the burden. It means a lot.

Thank you for seeing me.
It meant the world that you did.
I know the truth is
that you didn't really mean it,
But still,
I don't get that every day.

It changed my whole life.
A power I'm sure you
never knew you could have
Over someone like me,
But you did.
And you do to this day.
In some form, anyway.

You took me on a journey.
You pushed me
And were pushed right back.
I think you met your match
In that way.
It was my favorite thing to be.

It was beyond imagination.
Living it once, twice,
Any amount of times,
Never would have been enough.
And that's a shame.
The thing that made it worth doing
Is the thing that ultimately killed it.

I'll never really stop missing it.
It was too perfect
And I've accepted that.
It's a hell of a burden
To carry around
But I carry it always.

Seasonal Spam

like a novelty condiment
or some other one off
variety of pre-packaged food,
I was exciting to you in
the beginning, but I was
ultimately forgotten, left wasted
and unwanted on a shelf

"You pierce my soul."

Batteries Not Included

Love me so I can.
See me so I am.

Giles Corey (Pressed to Death)

If you need me, just call.

Stone.
Stone.
Stone.
Stone.

If you're feeling hopeless, reach out.

Stone.
Stone.
Stone.
Stone.

Day or night. Anytime.

Stone.
Stone.
Stone.
Stone.

Help is just a phone call away.

Stone.
Stone.
Stone.
Stone.

All you have to do is ask.

Stone.

Rock Bottom

Enough is enough
Wake the fuck up
Pick yourself up
Build yourself up
Give your own applause
Make yourself smile
Hold your own heart
Hear your own mind
See your own strength
Be your own strength
Open your own eyes
Face your own truth
Enough is enough
You are enough
It's beyond time
To start being enough.

State of the Disunion Address: Abridged

Things are complicated.
No longer easy or simple.
There was a brief happiness
and a lot of confusion
and loss and pain.
The loss is—astronomical.
To care so much and to be
entirely unable to connect
is a living nightmare.
It's like being stuck in the wrong timeline.

I remember a time when things were perfect.
So simple. Free of pressure. Wholesome.
My walls were gone.
I was open. I was comfortable.
The single best time of my life.
I wouldn't trade it for the world.

It was just what I needed
and that's what I really want.

Find your place of comfort.
Exist in peace.
Live within your own capacity.
I expect nothing more.

I love you just as you are.
Unconditionally.

Head to Toe

Today I dressed for my own funeral.
Ready, stoic, because in my experience,
What doesn't kill you just comes later,
Both reliable and unexpected,
Somehow unable to be prevented,
Despite always knowing, always feeling,
It is coming, is it coming, there it is.
Over, and over, and over again,
It becomes…tiresome.
Despite sighs, and rolling of eyes,
Dress up. Show up.
Feel it again.
Head to toe: Black.

Stability

You saved my life.
You continue to save my life.
I won't ever forget.

Making Mittens

Sitting and knitting,
knitting mittens,
mittens upon mittens,
pairs upon pairs,
for you,
so that your hands
may never be cold
for a moment.

Satisfied

If I seem intense, it's because I am.

If I seem vital, it's because
I am determined to live,
I am determined to love,
I feel directed to share
and connect my spirit
to the best of my ability
and for the greatest positive effect.

To feel is to know
in matters of the soul
and I know you are essential
in this journey

and I know

I am lost in you.

I want you to feel that like electricity
running with frantic tingles and burning warmth
from the back of your ear to your jawline
across your lips and down the sides of your neck
all the way to your fingertips and toes
and back again to set your heart on fire
in burning gasps until you quake
with energy like you've never known
and that you never want to forget

Until then, I am ready.
Until then, I am yours.
Only then am I satisfied.

_Pantoum_onium

when all reaches its limit
it retracts like a rubber band
pulling close, knocking over, crushing
all that has been gathered

it retracts like a rubber band
constricting air, blood, possibility
all that has been gathered
losing progress and starting again

constricting air, blood, possibility
recovery demands a new path
losing progress and starting over
until all reaches its limit

At the end of the day

So, even though
you were an absolutely
horrible, careless,
inconsiderate, juvenile
mother fucker,
I don't hold it against you.
I forgive you.
I feel like I should
say that once in a while.

Esoteric Dreaming

Pale moon? casting shadows
and tricks of light like desert dunes
twinkling at midnight

it sleeps in silence

Making sense of the darkness
and the delight within

Subtle Rise and Fall
suggesting the living and the alive

time and space constricts
in warmth and murmurs
until it shudders, quaking
cataclysmic

time stops and space ripples
in waves through the night
until calm
until dawn

The sunlight kisses my forehead
once, twice and warms
my fingertips and toes

till I rise, proud in my own skin.

Blindsided

Every single day of my life.
That's how often you cross my mind,
blindsided, like an ambush
of warm shivers up my spine,

The kind that make me
    put my head back
        close my eyes
            mouth open wide

The kind that make me
    release a
        shuddered   gasp

The kind that leaves me
    wanting you like nothing else

Even if nothing ever happens
Even if   anything and
    everything possible happens

I think you will always cross my mind,
every single day of my life,
blindsided, warm shivers up my spine
and that
    is more exciting
        than it has any right to be.

Solar Keratitis

to me, you were the sun
against all advice
against my advice
my life's light rose and set with you

your light persists, but burns
and I try to shut my eyes to it
but the pain pierces through

there is no shelter
no protection no respite
I burn, exposed to the elements

it is an agony I never expected
from the sun that warmed my heart
from the one that earned my trust
magnifying the pain by multitudes

it is unbearable
unchangeable
my life's light will rise and set with it
extinguished

"I am half agony, half hope."

Mourning #2

And we became I, I severed
trudging along in tall britches
to start my new life, free,
tending to wounds, published,
year delayed

Don't call it a comeback.

The Have and the Have-Not

It's a difficult thing to reconcile.
I miss you.
I miss you, but you're here.
I miss you, but you're not gone.
I miss you, but I still have you.
In some ways,
I have more of you than I had before,
but I still miss you.
It's a silly way to feel,
but it's very real
and very profound.

Another Brick

Once the victory conditions
have been established
there only remains
to build a strategy of attack

> But what if
> the path is dark and twisted

what if
the path is insurmountable

> what if
> the path is fraught with dangers

Surely staying back could be a choice
The comfort, the known, the old paths
Surely there is always tomorrow

> Before holding back,
> consider this sage advice
> once given to me
> by an old friend
> and now to you
> hold it true

Go today.
If you don't, tomorrow will seem a failure
(Though it may not be)
If you go, it's one more
Brick of Badassery
in this amazing person
you're continuing to become.

Win the fucking day.

Goddamn, thank you for everything

If there ever was
Going to be a sanctuary
Or a safe harbor
That could keep me
Calm, it would be
His arms holding me
Until the pain is gone

Low Tide

The wave pulled back
from the shoreline
and I'm not over it
I don't want to be over it
and I'm not ready to give up.

I never wanted to be in the ocean
nor only on land
but to walk my own path
as soft waves mix with
my footsteps and back again.
It is perfection.

ebb and flow
ebb and flow
one to appreciate the other
now in ebb

The wave is gone,
a safer place for me,
but I really just want it back.

So I wait in sand exposed,
yearning in patience,
but that tide is long overdue.

Snapshot
of the soufflé before the big, plopping tears fell
bringing it back down to Earth

I know it was real
I was there
For that snapshot of time
Just for a minute
When everything fell into place
Everything I never dreamed
Was right there
where I Never, ever,
Never expected to find it
And it was good
It set my heart alight
So bright
Up until that
Flash bulb burst
Leaving shadow
In the bone-dry world
Of *no I never*
I would never
No I didn't
It was misconstrued
I was confused
I mean I'm sorry
But no.
And I've got that
Snapshot burning
A twisted mural
Into my brain
Searing into my soul
Because I was there
I was there and it was real
Just for a minute
And it was truly
Gorgeous
In an "I can't take it back"
Kind of way
Just for me
I know it's me

And I'm not a fool
But I was there
And it was real for me
but all things <u>not</u> considered
it was real for you too
Just for a minute.

Freedom

I'm free.
I am—free,
but I'm like the
Statue of Liberty—

I still carry a torch.

Yelling at Glass

window pane
keeps me warm
protects me from the storm
and the rain
but clear shot to the pain

and I'm yelling at glass—
my heartbeat so fast
brings warmth to my soul
but it's cold to the touch
can't see me
won't hear me
but I love it so much
it's beautiful but dark
clear but opaque
I stay but might shatter
I change but might break

I'm yelling at glass—
but it breaks me
and it saves me
and it breaks me
but it saves me

yelling at glass.

I Yield

I yield
sometimes
and I yield today
deep down I know
when I put my heart away I know
when I open wide and peer through these eyes
without the aid of roses
I know
in the barest, coldest sense
in the most basic, truth-forward way
I know better
and I yield

Lost Found Poem

For much of the day, okay.
But overall not good at all.
I've been yearning for death.

I don't know how to talk about
this without scaring people

You sure you want to hear it?

It will be disturbing.

Every cell in my body is pleading for relief
and the overwhelming feeling is how much
better it would feel to be dead.

Consciousness is pain.

Outwardly I've been able to present in good
spirits and I've tried to be productive. But
inside those thoughts are screaming and
demanding attention.

I'm always feeling

Thanks. That is where I am.

Host

Welcome back.
I'll be your host tonight,
Fatal Parasite.
It's on the house.
Pry my eyes open
to force me to see
Pry my mind open
to force me to think
Pry my heart open
to force me to feel
I want to die.
I want to die.
I want to die.
It's all I know.
It's all I recognize.
It's all I expect.
It's all I am,

Until I am not.

"Tell me not that I am too late, that such
precious feelings are gone forever."

Twelve Pounds

Twelve pounds of shock and reeling
    Twelve pounds of resentment
Twelve pounds of heartbreak
    Twelve pounds of breaking hearts
Twelve pounds of wait
    Twelve pounds of don't be hasty
Twelve pounds of I forgive you
    Twelve pounds of let me change
Twelve pounds of processing
    Twelve pounds of promise me
Twelve pounds of one thing at a time
    Twelve pounds of apologize
Twelve pounds of we're there for you
    Twelve pounds of reconnection
Twelve pounds of no false hope
    Twelve pounds of no promises
Twelve pounds of I'm not interested
    Twelve pounds of I need to be alone
Twelve pounds of why not me?
    Twelve pounds of why not us?
Twelve pounds of care too much
    Twelve pounds of apathy
Twelve pounds of new friendship
    Twelve pounds of new self

It Ripples
An Interlude of Joy

That peach is bouncing.
It Ripples.
It's juicier than a concord grape.
Warm like a fresh baked pie.
I can see, hear, and feel the potential to drop a SLAP.
Gotta be sweet to the peach.
Avery is not from Georgia,
But she will shake a peach.
Ay Dios Mio.
She's a downright ducky shincracker.
She sounds like pink.
She smells like sweet yellow.
Yellow like a sunflower.
Yellow like the sun,
If the sun were sweet and warm and touchable,
And much smaller, and much easier to handle.
A heart only beats because she smiles.
The sparkly green eyes of adventure.
Like how the stars twinkle with madness.
She reaches out and brushes them with her fingertips.
Hank is fascinated by this being.
Hank will continue to be for a good long while.
Avery is a once-in-a-lifetime spunky little she-biscuit.
It is she who fills the pantry of life, guaranteed.
It is the peach who bounces in to say, "What's shakin' mama?"
Fresh baked, warm, juicy, sweet.

Triolet

My heart sets out to bring me home
and find the path to walk alone
and break the past and make me whole
my heart sets out to bring me home
and break away from what I've known
and break the bonds that aren't my own
my heart sets out to bring me home
and find the path to walk alone.

Something somewhat resembling a sonnet

For the first time, a chance to know myself
To see myself, define myself, brand new
To see through my own eyes and know it's real
To build upon the bricks under my feet
Without begging to be loved, as a crutch
To stand me up and act like I'm alive
Like a cardboard cutout selling bargains
But we, or I, don't need that anymore
I know my value and it's mine to own
Having taken the word of "George" to heart
After falling into the dark waters
I've found footing even on sliding stones
My gold: my heart, my soul, my life stands firm
I can't go back. I won't go back. I'm here.

How to make your guests feel at home
Hosting friends as a novice, 37-year-old

Absolutely killer
apartment warming party.
10 out of 10.
I take five minutes
to have a friend
help me put my
clean bedsheets on
so my drunk ass
has somewhere to sleep
and when we come back
the place is empty?
Aside from literally everyone
shouting on the balcony.
But I'm told I should
not let it bother me
that everyone left
pissed off because
it was a great time.
10 out of 10
Apartment warming party.

XXL

After I set forth to find myself, I found myself
bound by my own feelings to
care rather than
dare to walk away.
Even though I live apart now, I
find that we are closer than ever,
granted I don't know that we ever
had it
in us over the last five years. We
just went through the motions,
knowing but not knowing
love shouldn't feel like this and
maybe we lost the thread somewhere
near the beginning,
or we never really started, and
perhaps those years didn't really happen to us. I
question whether they
really should have.
So here we are on
the other side of it,
understanding each other for the
very first time,
wondering why we waited so long. You're an
ex ex now.
You're worth another chance. At this point, I have almost
zero hesitation.

Batteries Not Needed

I love. I am.
I see. I can.

Translation

Let me understand it, the truth.
And get here, to the bed, and speak more.
Here all of us are mourning.
As we wake in the morning.

It's about vastly living.
Exactly growing.
In my room, all I've seen, how he, over me, has built,
A moment.

If all seems, how he,
the broken, and standing over me, felt,
How the door did stand open,
Like talking late felt like what he keeps,
Over this thing. "Stop." Goddamn.

Let me, get around it, the truth.
Speak more or stop the mourning.
In the morning,
And in the mention of feelings,
And the bed,
And the grass,
What he, over me, meant.

Bad Advice Out of Context
A reflection on the poetry of Erin Hanson

"What if I fall?"
Let's see. Chances are, I'm falling.
I have no wings, no aviation device,
No parachute, which would only make me fall slower.
I will not be flying. I can tell you that much.
And don't call me your darling.

I would have less of a gripe
if people would quote your entire poem,
in context, but they never do.
It's only ever about being okay to fall
because they might just fly.

They will not.

The quotes are always missing the metaphor
about freedom waiting for us
on the breeze, and as someone
who has experienced freedom
and the danger of failure

I'd like to believe I can relate,
but I can't. Because if failure is falling,
I have fallen, but I have taken my injuries
and walked away. As far as I know
there was never an option to fly instead.

So, my darling, I did fall. I did not fly
into the freedom waiting for me
on the breezes of the sky.

I fell face first, and tumbled,
landed with a direct gaze
on what was behind me,
but I am now here, in the freedom
that was waiting for me.

Oyster

The future is in my hands today
To direct and follow my heart
To seek and find and not find
To speak and not be heard
To build and to break
To act in chains
To stumble
and fall
down

Still

it is so still
still like silent
still like peaceful
still like patient
still like faith
still like feeling
still like knowing
still like loving you, still

It is so.
Still.

Plus One

Boredom turns to pain in a single breath,
passing the time turns to passing this life,
anything to kill this goddamn feeling,
the agony is everything, the agony is all,
Love pales beside, hope defers to dark,
when all the dust settles, all is cold,

The heart, the body aches within the cold,
fighting for the will to take a breath,
nothing feels so far away as life,
nothing feels as impossible as feeling,
numbness seeps in to overtake all,
comfort comes unexpected in the dark,

There is peace and safety in the dark,
in the quiet, things don't feel so cold,
finally, there is space to take a breath,
a renewed warmth to living life,
an overflow of positive feeling,
So eager for the possibility of all,

Strength rebuilt to defeat it all,
To find every light within the dark,
to create warmth to thaw the cold,
To fill lungs deeply with every breath,
Grateful for every minute of life,
So desperate to hold on to this feeling,

Sincere effort to embrace all feeling,
to face and own the pain of it all,
to live free in the light and dark,
to thrive in warmth as well as cold,
to accept uncertainty and halted breath,
to head full on into the harshness of life,

Bleak and uncaring and cold, this life,
so much is clear punishment for feeling,
easy to question the point of it all,
the apathy lives entirely in the dark,

and it leaves the heart feeling so cold,
yearning for that last painful breath,

So stand for life, for now, and brace for feeling,
push through it all, for now, and kneel in the dark,
wait in the cold, for now, and lean on that
                              painful,
                                    enduring breath.

        To carry through to the next.

How was your day?

It's an earbuds-and-shades kind of day,
a let-the-air-dry-your-tears kind of day,
a walking-with-a-soundtrack-like-a-movie kind of day,

a life-half-over kind of day,
a heart-half-broken kind of day,
a losing-my-mind-because-we-haven't-spoken kind of day,

once-again-checking-that-you-don't-hate-me kind of day,
a half-kind-word-away-from-weeping kind of day,
a hugging-my-arms-to-keep-from-shaking kind of day,

a see-right-through-me kind of day,
a run-right-through-me kind of day,
the kind of day that defines, confines,
reminds, and resigns me
to the white flag,
the cold, sad persistence of the Never.

How are you?

All I think of ever
"All I think of ever is that I love you." -F. Scott Fitzgerald

My god, is that the truth.
I am never alone
with that fact beside me,
ever-present so long
as I still breathe,
and I still breathe
for the sake of
loving you always.

"I have loved none but you."

Afterword

Again, I do it.
Again, I do it.
Again, I do it.
Suicidal and euphoric.
I break and break my heart.
Like a rabbit, my soul mates
with fate
with serendipity.
My luck pushing a
romantic, hopeless
ship jumper,
heartbreaker,
chronic LTR
junkie of dopamine,
limerence addict.
Knees ticklish.
I can remember so far.
Crazy boys.
They call me.
My own cycle breaking
my attempt at
what precedes.

ABOUT THE AUTHOR

Hannah Wilkinson is an independent poet currently existing and writing in Nebraska. She is trying as hard as humanly possible to find the stability and strength necessary to move forward in this life. Poetry is her natural mode of expressing what needs to be expressed for good or bad. If we accept the premise that she has something important to say, then she firmly believes this is the path that has been provided by the Universe for her to seek happiness until the road runs out. She hopes readers can get something out of the experience as well.

 She has previously published a collection of short stories and poems titled *Unto the Breach*. Upon publishing this collection, work will begin on something very special that is currently in the milling over phase. We hope you get to see it.

May you have peace in your heart.